Introduction

If you're a seasoned pickleball
pro or a curious newbie just dipping
your paddle in the pickleball pool,
you've come to the right place. You'll
discover a treasure trove of words,
phrases, and excuses that are as
colorful and diverse as the players
who wield those paddles.

Pickleball, a sport that has been gaining popularity across the globe, is more than just a game; it's a community, a camaraderie, and a source of enjoyment. And at the heart of that community, lies a language all its own.

Part 1

Pickleball Lingo: A-Z Guide to Slang and Fun Vocabulary

In the world of sports, each game has its own unique language, a lexicon of words, phrases, and inside jokes that bind players together and create a culture all their own. The sport of Pickleball is no exception. Welcome to the whimsical and wacky world of pickleball lingo, where "dinking" is an art form, "the kitchen" is a forbidden realm, and the "Put-Away" is a thing of beauty.

Pickle:

This term is often used humorously to refer to the pickleball itself.

Bagel:

Winning a game 11-0...

...or losing a game 0-11

Giggle Paddle:

A term sometimes used for a beginner-level paddle or a paddle that produces amusing or unpredictable results

Kitchen:

Also known as the "non-volley zone," it's the area near the net where players are not allowed to volley the ball.

Put-Away:

A powerful shot intended to win the point, typically used to finish a rally.

Golden Retriever:

A player who is quick and skilled at returning balls, often diving or making impressive saves.

Dink:

A Soft and low shot that just clears the net and lands in the opponent's non-volley zone. Dinking is all about control and placement.

Ernie:

A shot where a player runs around the non-volley zone to hit the ball on the opposite side of the net, typically executed with a forehand volley.

Granny Shot:

A high, arcing shot resembling a basketball granny shot, often used to clear the net and place the ball precisely.

Fishing:

A term used to describe hitting high and deep lobs repeatedly to push opponents back and create an offensive opportunity.

No Man's Land:

The area on the court between the baseline and the non-volley zone. It can be a tricky position to play from.

Kitchen Line Hugger:

A player who tends to stay as close to the non-volley line as possible, using it to their strategic advantage.

Shotgun:

A powerful and aggressive shot that aims to overwhelm the opponent.

Rainmaker:

A high and heavy topspin shot that arcs dramatically and can be difficult to return.

The Switch:

A strategy where players on the serving team may switch positions during the game, often to confuse the returner.

Kitchen Crawl:

When a player approaches the kitchen line and "crawls" along it, looking for an opportunity to make an aggressive shot or volley.

Heckle Paddle:

A joking reference to a paddle that is perceived as noisy or disruptive on the court.

Brick Wall:

A player who has excelling defensive skills and is challenging to get the ball past.

Wooden Spoon:

An affectionate term for a beginner or someone that is new to the game of pickleball.

Corkscrew:

A spinning or curving shot, often achieved with a side-spin or backspin, making it challenging to predict the ball's path.

Chicken Wing:

A technique where a player's elbow is extended when hitting the ball, resembling a chicken wing.

Bingo Bango Bongo:

A lighthearted exclamation often used when players score points or make winnings shots.

Happy Feet:

A player who frequently shuffles their feet, often indicating nervousness or anticipation of the opponent's shot.

Paddle Jockey:

A person who constantly switches between different paddles in search of the perfect one for their game.

Around-the-Post (ATP):

A spectacular shot where a player hits the ball around the net post and into the opponents court, often used in doubles play.

Pickle-tegrity:

Quality of being honest and having moral principles as it relates to the game of pickleball. Calling truthful shots, keeping honest score, etc.

Falafel:

A shot that falls short due to hitting the ball without any power.

Cheeseball:

A shot that is easy or straightforward that an opening ends up missing.

Mystery Meat:

A term that refers to a shot that's difficult to predict or return effectively.

Paddle Dropper:

A player known for their ability to execute successful drop shots, often frustrating their opponents.

POACH:

When a player on the non-serving team crosses the centerline to hit the ball before the intended recipient can do so.

Golden Set:

A game where a player or team wins without allowing the opponents to score a single point.

Misdirect:

A shot that tricks the opponent by appearing to go in one direction but then changing direction mid-flight.

Spin Doctor:

A player who excels at putting spin on the ball, making it difficult for their opponents to predict the trajectory.

Clean Winner:

A shot that results in a point for the hitter without the opponent making any effort to return it.

Side Out:

When the serving team loses the serve and the opposing team gets a chance to serve.

King of the Court:

A fun format where players compete to stay on the court as long as possible by winning points and games.

Soft Game:

A style of play that emphasizes control and finesse over power, often involving dinking and drop shots.

Hairpin Shot:

A shot that follows a curved trajectory, typically used to clear the net and land in the opponent's court.

Blinker:

A player who takes their eye off the ball for just a moment, resulting in a mistake.

Rainmaker:

A high lob shot that goes high into the air and seemingly disappears into the clouds before landing in the opponent's court.

Kitchen Police:

Players who are vigilant about enforcing the non-volley zone rules and catching any infractions.

Windmill:

A fast and exaggerated swing, often associated with beginners or overzealous players.

Eclipse Shot:

A shot that lands very close to the baseline, making it difficult for opponents to judge and return.

Down the Middle Solves the Riddle:

Hitting a shot in between your opponents and neither of them hit it.

Salmon:

A player who is constantly moving backward during the game, resembling a salmon swimming upstream.

Rally:

An exchange of shots between the two teams during a point.

Foot Fault:

A violation that occurs when a player's foot crosses the baseline during the serve.

Lighthouse:

A player who consistently serves aces, acting as a guiding light for their team.

One-and-Done:

A game or match that ends quickly, often due to a significant skill gap between players or teams.

Rally Scoring:

A scoring system where points can be won on both the serving and receiving team's serves.

Roll Shot:

A shot that is hit with backspin and moves unpredictably when it bounces.

Drop Shot:

A softly hit shot that lands and is intentionally hit close to the net.

Half Volley:

A Shot where the ball is hit just after it bounces, often used to return low shot types.

Bread and Butter Shot:

A player's favorite and most reliable shot.

Frying Pan Grip:

The Western pickleball grip. It resembles how you may hold a frying pan.

Dink Fest:

A long rally that consists of mainly dink shots near the net.

Getting Pickled:

Losing and not scoring a point.

Tweener:

Hitting a shot between your legs.

Erne:

Jumping over your side of the kitchen into the outside of the court and hitting a shot downward while you're in the air or standing in the legal spot outside the court.

Nutmeg:

Hitting a ball through your opponent's legs.

Shake n' Bake:

When the third shot in a doubles match is a "drive" and the other player rushes to the net to hit a put-a-way.

Ace:

When a player hits a serve, and the returning player does not get a paddle on it.

Body Bag:

A shot that hit's your opponent's body.

Pedicure:

A shot that hit's your opponent's foot.

Manicure:

A shot that hits your opponent's hand.

Banger:

Someone who continuously drives the ball and hits the ball very hard at their opponent.

Flapjack:

This is a shot that that should bounce before you hit it.

Dinner:

A winning shot that is a "dink."

Part 2

Pickleball Excuses: The Ability to Explain Your Way to Victory

Welcome to the section where the sun is perpetually in your eyes, the wind is always at the wrong speed, and the court itself seems to conspire against your winning shots.

"The Sun Was in My Eyes"

"My Shoes are Too Tight"

"I Just Ate Before I Started Playing"

"The Wind!"

"I'm Playing the Long Game"

"I Was Testing the Laws of Physics"

"The Court is Crooked"

"There's a Hole in my Paddle"

"The Ball Was Too Shiny"

"You Guys Got the Lucky Side"

"I Wasn't Really Trying"

"I Got Lost in Thought"

"My Shadow Got in the Way"

"I Was Channeling My Inner Sloth"

"You Must've Paid the Net"

"I'm Pretty Tired"

"Oh – This is a New Paddle!"

"My Grip is Starting to Wear"

"I Wasn't Ready"

"I Was Still Warming Up"

"Oof – My Pickleball Elbow is Acting Up"

"The Ball Bounces Differently Here"

"I Was Trying Out a New Shot"

"I Haven't Played in a While"

"I'm Not Used to Playing With These Balls"

"I Was Practicing My Lob Shot"

"My Grip Was Slipping"

"These Are New Shoes"

"You Were Getting Lucky"

"The Spin Threw Me Off"

"I Forgot to Stretch"

"I Couldn't See the Ball"

"I Got Caught in a Butterfly Stampede"

"That Was My Last Mistake"

"OK – THAT Was my Last Mistake"

"I Thought There Was a Ball Coming Over Here"

"I Thought I Heard "Ball!""

"It's My First Game"

"It's My First Time Playing in a While"

"The Net is Too High!"

"This Court is Too Slippery"

"The Net is Too Loose!"

"Are These Lines Regulation?"

"Is This Net USAPA Approved?"

"This Court Looks Small"

Looks at Paddle Confused

"My Paddle Has a Mind of Its Own"

"Just Shaking Off the Cobwebs"

"If I was That Tall…"

"My Shoe Was Untied!"

"My Opponent is Too Good"

"I'm So Used to Playing Indoor"

"I'm So Sore From…"

"I Was Trying to Save Energy"

"This Must Be an Indoor Ball"

"I Had a Late Night..."

"I Think it Was Out"

"I Think My Paddle Has a Dead Spot"

"I Was Just Being Lazy"

"Now I'll Start Trying"

Made in United States
Orlando, FL
09 December 2024

55240857R10029